DOING
TIME

A Spiritual Survival Guide

JONATHAN AITKEN
& EDWARD SMYTH

LION

Text copyright © 2021 Jonathan Aitken and Edward Smyth

This edition copyright © 2021 Lion Hudson IP Limited

The right of Jonathan Aitken and Edward Smyth to be identified as the authors of this work has been asserted by them in accordance with the Copyright, Designs and Patents Act 1988.

All rights reserved. No part of this publication may be reproduced or transmitted in any form or by any means, electronic or mechanical, including photocopy, recording, or any information storage and retrieval system, without permission in writing from the publisher.

Published by
Lion Books
www.lionhudson.com

Part of the SPCK Group

SPCK, 36 Causton Street, London, SW1P 4ST

ISBN 978 0 74598 148 2
e-ISBN 978 0 74598 149 9

First edition 2021

Acknowledgments

Scripture quotations marked NIV taken from The Holy Bible, New International Version® NIV® Copyright © 1973 1978 1984 2011 by Biblica, Inc. TM. Used by permission. All rights reserved worldwide.

Scripture quotations marked NRSV are from The New Revised Standard Version Bible: Anglicized Edition, copyright © 1989, 1995 National Council of the Churches of Christ in the United States of America. Used by permission. All rights reserved worldwide.

Scripture quotations marked ESV are from The Holy Bible, English Standard Version® (ESV®) copyright © 2001 by Crossway, a publishing ministry of Good News Publishers. All rights reserved.

Scriptures quotations marked GNB are from the Good News Bible © 1994 published by the Bible Societies/HarperCollins Publishers Ltd UK, Good News Bible© American Bible Society 1966, 1971, 1976, 1992. Used with permission.

Scriptures quotations marked KJV are from The Authorized (King James) Version. Rights in the Authorized Version are vested in the Crown. Reproduced by permission of the Crown's patentee, Cambridge University Press.

Scripture quotations marked NIrV are taken from the Holy Bible, New International Reader's Version®, NIrV® Copyright © 1995, 1996, 1998, 2014 by Biblica, Inc.™ Used by permission of Zondervan. All rights reserved worldwide. www.zondervan.com The "NIrV" and "New International Reader's Version" are trademarks registered in the United States Patent and Trademark Office by Biblica, Inc.™

Page 44, lyrics of 'If I Were a Butterfly' © 1974 Mission Hills Music (Adm Song Solutions www.songsolutions.org) All rights reserved. Used by permission.

Every effort has been made to trace copyright holders and to obtain permission for the use of copyright material. The publisher apologizes for any errors or omissions and would be grateful to be notified of any corrections that should be incorporated in future reprints of this book.

A catalogue record for this book is available from the British Library

Printed and bound in the UK, February 2022, LH57

JONATHAN AITKEN is an ex-MP, ex-cabinet minister, and ex-prisoner. After pleading guilty to telling a lie on oath in a libel action, he served an eighteen-month prison sentence in 1989. An Oxford graduate in law and theology, he is a well-known broadcaster, author, and journalist. He was ordained in 2018 and is now serving as a voluntary prison chaplain at HMP Pentonville and as an assistant priest at St Matthew's Westminster.

EDWARD SMYTH served a brief prison sentence in 2015 at the age of twenty-four. He has since acquired a master's degree in criminology from Oxford and has built a career in criminal justice. He currently works for the Forward Trust and is researching part-time for a doctorate in theology, focusing on prison chaplaincy, at Durham University.

Acknowledgments

JONATHAN

I acknowledge with gratitude the prisoners, the prison officers, the chaplains, and other staff I met during the seven months I spent serving my sentence in HMPs Belmarsh, Standford Hill, and Elmley in 1999–2000. I also thank my colleagues among the chaplains, the prison officers, the managers, and the governors of HMP Pentonville where I have served as a voluntary chaplain since 2018. This book has greatly benefitted from the experiences I have shared with them all.

EDWARD

To individually thank all those who deserve it would double the length of this book. If they don't know who they are, then I have failed as a friend to the same extent that they have excelled. Some must be mentioned by name, though: Aileen, David, Ed, Anne, Tristan, Niamh, Patrick and Lydia, Edd and Carys, Esther and my marvellous godchildren Bea and Teddy, Fr Peter Groves, Mthr Mel Marshall, Fr Philip Chester, and those mentioned in this book whose names I have changed – I can't express what I owe you. Thank you also to Fr Jonathan Aitken whose patience, wise counsel, generosity, and friendship have been a very real blessing from God. His ministry is a gift to many, both behind bars and on the out, and an inspiration to me.

Contents

Introduction

This book is written by two former prisoners.

It came from a conversation between two people who remember vividly the slamming of the cell door at the end of a day which began in the dock, and the storm of emotions which accompanied that experience.

One of us fell from grace in the most public manner imaginable – from the Cabinet table in 10 Downing Street to prison cell, financial ruin, and divorce in a few short years.

The other was barely two years into his first job before behaving so appallingly that he found himself stopped in his tracks by the flash of a police officer's warrant card. The future he had imagined for himself was swept away in an instant, and he could blame no one but himself.

The experience of a prison sentence sent us both back to university – both trying to understand something about our own experiences and about the very different lives we now found ourselves leading. One studied for a degree in theology, the other in criminology.

This book is for anyone who finds themselves the wrong side of the locked door. But although you may find advice to make your sentence easier, this is not really a book designed to answer questions. Nor is it a book which claims to know exactly how you may be feeling at any particular time.

If the experience of prison taught the two of us anything, it is that your sentence will be an intensely private affair, during which you will experience the full range of human emotion. There is no map for you to follow, because everyone is different. But one thing did keep us going. Both of us went through our sentences confident that God was with us.

This book is also for anyone connected to someone in prison. Whether you are family, friend, acquaintance, or concerned church member, this book is for you.

This is also a book for those who are professionally involved in the care and custody of prisoners.

Beginning in 2018, a significant number of new, young prison officers have begun their careers. They came as a solution to misguided "austerity" cuts which resulted in nearly 30% of the entire prison workforce being encouraged to take early retirement in 2015–2016. This serious mistake had to be reversed by an emergency £500 million recruitment drive of over 2,500 new officers. Those new officers are, of course, inexperienced, but they are also open to new thinking. This fresh blood in the Prison Service has been further strengthened by hundreds of new officers who have joined under the "Unlocked Graduates" scheme which started in 2017. This has been highly successful.

So, whether you are professionally concerned with prisoners, or a prisoner yourself, or a member of a prisoner's family, or just vaguely wondering whether you should feel curious or compassionate toward those who find themselves locked up, we hope the experiences of two ex-prisoners, and their reflections on those experiences, will prove of use.

And for those on the outside, whether someone you know and love is inside, or whether you've never given all that much thought to those living and working behind the walls and wire, we hope this is more than a quick trip behind those walls. Society likes not to think about its prisons all that often; people of faith can and should do better.

We hope, then, that the memories, reflections, and prayers that you will find in the following pages will help you, whoever you are, on your spiritual journey through a reality which, somehow, has been touched by prison.

You are in our prayers; please keep us in yours.

JONATHAN & EDWARD

Chapter 1
The First Night

"The darker the night, the brighter the stars," wrote the Russian poet Apollon Maykov. "The deeper the grief, the closer is God!"

The first night in prison is a time of grief; and despite the noise and the confusion it will be a time of profound loneliness.

Almost everyone who has experienced it describes it as the worst night of their sentence, and even the worst of their lives. God may feel very distant that night, no matter the strength of one's faith. But he is not distant – far from it.

God may feel very distant that night, no matter the strength of one's faith.

There is no handbook for surviving a first night. There is no way of avoiding the doubt and shame and fear which will form part of those dark hours. But the following reflections come from two people who have journeyed through this valley of tears. It is a well-trodden path, no matter how utterly alone you feel.

Stale reassurances that "things will get better" are going to be of little use to you as you read these words, as a new prisoner, as a worried family member, or as a friend. But we both found some comfort from this passage, Psalm 139:7–12 (NIV):

Where can I go from your Spirit?
Where can I flee from your presence?
If I go up to the heavens, you are there;
if I make my bed in the depths, you are there.
If I rise on the wings of the dawn,
if I settle on the far side of the sea,
even there your hand will guide me,
your right hand will hold me fast.
If I say, "Surely the darkness will hide me
and the light become night around me,"
even the darkness will not be dark to you;
the night will shine like the day,
for darkness is as light to you.

Reflections

JONATHAN

A first night in custody is likely to be a shocking experience to most new arrivals. This is a strange and alien world with its own rituals, customs, language, and way of life. How should you handle it?

Entering prison is both an outward and an inward journey. The externals are testing. The noise levels can pound the eardrums with the shouting, the banging and clanging of iron barred gates. Then there are the despair and anger which flow through the reception area known as "The Cage".

The rituals are strange. Strip searching (usually done in a relatively dignified way); fingerprinting; mugshot photography; recording (and often confiscating) your possessions in a "prop" book; and being allocated a cell (plus a fellow prisoner to share it) can all be difficult experiences. But they are the easy bit.

What goes on inside your head, your heart, and your soul will prove a far more challenging inner journey. To put it mildly you will be having a down day. Perhaps it will feel like the worst day of your life. But do not despair. Experience shows that you can get through your first night as a prisoner.

Indeed you may be pleasantly surprised to discover that the milk of human kindness flows through the "new arrivals" wing. There will be plenty of trained fellow inmates to help you find your feet. The officers you will meet during the first few hours of your sentence will probably be quite kind. Don't be afraid to ask them for help and guidance. They want you to settle in peacefully. Prison staff are in authority but they are not your enemies. Treat them politely, respectfully, and considerately and they will treat you well too.

Do not be afraid. You are extremely unlikely to encounter hostility, let alone violence. Move cautiously at first but be willing to extend or accept the hand of friendship. As your eyes start to get accustomed to the landscape of prison you will find that decent, kindly people vastly outnumber the unpleasant characters. Be ready to play your part in contributing to a friendly, mutually respectful spirit.

Almost everyone has a spiritual dimension to their lives, however much they have suppressed it or ignored it. Prison is not a bad place to explore the part of your being which is called the soul. Yes, you have hit a rock-bottom low point. But you *will* recover from it and rebuild your life.

Be willing to extend or accept the hand of friendship.

You are "in the depths" right now but perhaps if you listen to the spiritual whispers in your soul you may begin to hear some answers to your immediate problem.

One of the most celebrated prisoners of the nineteenth century, Oscar Wilde, who served his time in Pentonville, Wandsworth, and Reading jails, wrote a book about his experiences titled *De Profundis*, Latin for "Out of the depths". Those words were taken from the opening verse of Psalm 130, sometimes called "The Prisoner's Psalm", which runs:

> *Out of the depths I cry to you, LORD;*
> *LORD, hear my voice. (NIV)*

If you can borrow a Bible, read this short psalm in full because it has much to say to any prisoner about God's mercy, forgiveness, peace, and grace. It advises prayer, patience, and a sense of hope. If you realize on your first night in jail that you need these gifts, you are already travelling in the right direction.

I had a difficult start to my first night because there had been so much publicity (back in 1999 a cabinet minister going to jail was big news – things have changed a bit since!) that the inmates of HMP Belmarsh did a lot of scary shouting about me. Some of their threats about what they would like to do to various parts of my body when they met a hated "Tory cabinet minister" on the wing sounded alarming. But as most of these shouters were "on the tackle" (on drugs) their noise meant nothing. All was peaceful and friendly on the wing the following morning.

Yet by a strange coincidence those threats sent me dipping into my Bible, which is when I stumbled upon Psalm 130. (The Psalms form part of the Old Testament, and Jesus used them as a prayer book.) As I read and reread it, starting from that first line, "Out of the depths I cry to you, LORD", a warm wave of reassurance flooded over me. Suddenly, I realized that I was not as lonely, scared, helpless, or vulnerable as I had thought. The author of the psalm had been there before me. Some 3,000 years earlier he had experienced despair like mine. He had found a route to climb out of his depths with God's help, and he had described that route in beautiful but realistic poetry.

The author of the psalm had recognized that a climb out of the depths is likely to be a long, tough haul. There are no quick fixes. There can be no true repentance without pain. It takes courage to be sorry. After sinning against God, restoring fellowship with him can be a slow process. The psalmist wrote about waiting for forgiveness:

I wait for the LORD, my soul waits,
and in his word I hope;
my soul waits for the LORD
more than those who watch for the morning.
(Psalm 130:5–6, NRSV)

As I read these lines I had no problem in identifying with those watchmen. The months ahead of me were bound to be full of testing, watchful nights. I was going through one of them right then. Yet I sensed that how I waited was going to be important. The final stanza of the psalm promised unfailing love and full redemption. They were worth waiting for.

Thinking about these two rewards, love and redemption, drove away my first-night fears. All of a sudden, I was able to pray, and I started to accept my situation. Then I fell into a peaceful sleep which lasted for the next seven hours.

May you sleep well, and prayerfully, on your first night as a prisoner.

EDWARD

There are perhaps three contenders for the worst night of my life. One: the doorbell waking me to the news of my mother's death.

Another terrible night followed the day I had been arrested. The police had released me on bail. I lay in bed, the stillness of the night throwing into sharp relief the chaos of my mind, and of my life. Staring blankly at the ceiling and listening to the trains running through the cutting at the foot of the garden, my thoughts turned to whether those trains might carry me, not to London as they had so often in the past, but away more permanently – away from my responsibilities, away from the knowledge of my actions, and away from the life in which I would face their inevitable consequences. God was difficult to find that night.

The first night spent in a prison cell is the worst, though. The worst of my life; the worst in the lives of most people who've experienced the unique swirl of emotions it engenders: terror, confusion, foreboding, abandonment.

When the cell door slams shut you start the job of processing the events of the years, months, and day which led you to that point.

Central to that constellation of feelings is uncertainty. When the cell door slams shut you start the job of processing the events of the years, months, and day which led you to that point. This can be tough, because all those things which define our lives – which form the framework within which we operate and by which we define who we are – have been removed and not, as yet, replaced.

My own first night in prison will remain burned into my memory for the rest of my life. Looking back, it has taken on the quality of a dream: appalling, of course, but lent a certain farcical quality by my cellmate for that night, James.

James and I were, we would discover over the coming weeks, in similar positions. Roughly the same age, we were both experiencing prison for the first and – as we often hoped – only time.

That first night, James was not in a good way. I had first encountered him in the holding cell as we were being processed into the prison. He was sitting alone, weeping. We spoke for maybe ten minutes before he was led away to be stripped, searched, and issued with the standard prison clothing which all new prisoners wear for the first few weeks. Some hours later, I was shown to the cell which became my new bedroom, living space, and toilet. In it was James. Still weeping.

It is not a comfortable thing to admit, but James's evident distress helped me. I spent a long time talking with him about his life, his family, and his fear that other prisoners would discover his homosexuality. This helped me not to think about the rubble of my own life, the wreckage of my family relationships, and my worries about whether my partner would be able to cope with my imprisonment.

Crucially, it helped me to avoid dealing with the guilt for the actions which had sent me to prison, and the harm I had caused by them, which had been coldly illustrated to me in court earlier that day. That would come later.

James and I had to quickly get to know each other. Few things encourage stronger relationships than being forced to use an unscreened toilet less than a metre from another man's bed.

We were very open with each other from the start about which of the other's habits we found difficult. (I had decided to put up with James's smoking: I preferred to stick with a smoking cellmate with whom I got on than risk the reverse.) The worst bit was his inability to go to sleep without the television on. So that first night, as James finally drifted off into a fitful, restless sleep and I was left on the top bunk with my own thoughts, the soundtrack to my private despair was *Rocky*.

I so wish it had been a verse from the Bible which had given me comfort in the orange glow of the outside lights but, again, that would come later. Instead, as so often, it was a fictional character whose story spoke to me most profoundly. But I'm not going to tell you what it was that Rocky said which resonated with me so powerfully: my thoughts on that first night will be wildly different from yours, and it's fairly unlikely *Rocky* is also going to be on the television when you spend your first night in prison!

But there is a point to me telling you this. In the early stages of a rekindled – or new – relationship with God it can be tempting to think that the only way to think about or talk about him is through Bible verses and using "religious language"; that you can do without novels or television programmes; and that drawing parallels between those things and God is silly or somehow offensive. It's not true. Don't be afraid of learning from books, films, magazines, and the like. We can learn so much about ourselves and about God from other people, even if they're fictional. So, as much as I thought that terrible night that I ought to be feeling the urge to turn to the Bible, God worked with what I'd given him and spoke to me through the improbable – bizarre, even! – mouthpiece of Rocky. God often speaks quietly, or unexpectedly, or through unlikely channels. Keep listening out.

You are not alone

These are two very different experiences of a first night. Your first night, or your loved one's, will be as different again. But the tough times you face head-on through the small hours of the morning can and will, as with all tough times, be used by God.

You are not alone, however much you may feel alone. Martin Luther said, "It is in our pain and in our brokenness that we come closest to Christ." If we cry out to him in our prayers, he will come rushing to meet us. This happens every day to those who are in any kind of trouble, sadness, crisis, sickness, imprisonment, or any other adversity, and who reach out to Jesus.

The tough times you face head-on through the small hours of the morning can and will, as with all tough times, be used by God.

With him, you are stronger than you ever thought possible. With him, you will become stronger still as you pass through the refining fire of this night.

Be assured of our prayers for you, safe in the knowledge that "Tears may flow in the night, but joy comes in the morning" (Psalm 30:5, GNB).

Compassionate God,

Be with me this night in my fear and despair.

Be with those for whom I care,
and who care for me.

Come close to me as I face a new future,
fill me with your Holy Spirit, and walk with
me through this new landscape.

Grant that I may see your face in those I meet,

and that the flickering candle of my faith
might burn bright in these dark hours.

In Jesus' name,

Amen.

Chapter 2
Coming to Terms

No matter how well prepared you are for the possibility of a prison sentence, the reality of finding yourself on the wrong side of a locked door will be a shock.

It will be a shock to the senses, surely, but it will also be a more profound sort of shock.

There is the shock of having your life upended, with the disruption of all the routines and habits you have spent decades forming.

The reality of finding yourself on the wrong side of a locked door will be a shock.

There is the shock of suddenly finding it very difficult to see beyond the next few days, or months, or years.

There is the shock, possibly, of realizing that you are the sort of person who goes to prison... even when perhaps you'd been denying that particular reality until only a few hours earlier.

Riding out that shock and coming to terms with these new realities is a crucial, often painful, step. But it is the only way in which the potential for your prison sentence to be a positive, productive time can be realized.

Reflections

JONATHAN

As you start your sentence you will feel you have hit rock bottom. This experience may seem to be the lowest point of your life. That is probably true.

However, no prisoner needs to stay marooned at rock bottom. Yes, you are in the depths, but you can lift out of the depths if you make one or two practical and spiritual moves that are covered by the title of this chapter, "Coming to Terms".

Here are one or two suggestions on how to do this.

A good first move is to stop being in denial. Many prisoners (including me!) spend a huge amount of effort before being jailed denying their wrongdoing, fibbing to their friends and families, telling lies in court, and generally putting on a mask of deceit. That phase is over, but will you recognize it?

Staying in denial is a massive obstacle to coming to terms with reality. During my early days in HMP Belmarsh I was warned to take no notice of Prisoner X, because he was a "Double Richard".

"What's that?" I asked.

A more experienced prisoner explained to me that Richard the Third = Bird; that Bird = sentence; so a "Double Richard" was a man who was serving his sentence twice over because he was consumed by the bitterness of being in denial. Prisoner X was one of the least attractive characters I had ever met, because of his snarling, whingeing protests about his unfair treatment. I resolved never to follow his example and to stop my own denials about some of the twists and turns in my own saga which still left me with a grievance. So I flushed my grumblings, grievances, and denials down the loo and got on with prison life. This was a good move.

When you are out of denial you can get into hope. Hope is a fragile and rare plant in prison but it can be nurtured in practical ways. A good way to start this process is by trying to give other people hope or at least a word of good cheer or a smile. Once you start engaging with others on the wing, life starts to look up.

❝

Once you start engaging with others on the wing, life starts to look up.

Humour and humanity are crucial ingredients in a prison journey. So is a willingness to listen to other people's stories. Above all you should try to offer a touch of kindness to those who are down and distressed. The nineteenth-century Australian poet Adam Lindsay Gordon wrote the lines:

Life is mostly froth and bubble,
Two things stand like stone,
Kindness in another's trouble,
Courage in your own.

It is possible, indeed probable, that you will not feel at all courageous as you start your sentence. In the strange unfamiliar world of planet prison your fears may multiply. Prison can be a pressure cooker of an environment in which small problems become big problems, big problems become dramas, and dramas can grow into disasters, even catastrophes.

Much of this is in the mind, so a prisoner trying to come to terms with their situation should seek to calm their anxieties. This is easier said than done, particularly if worries are growing about the family you have left behind, or if you are adversely affected by the pressures of prison life such as noise, disagreeable neighbours on your wing, or sleeplessness.

I coped with these pressures in two ways. Outwardly, I tried to be pleasant, agreeable, and helpful to everyone I encountered. Inwardly, I found strength in prayer.

I was lucky in my outward journey. I was not so crass as to mount what is called "a charm offensive" or to make myself the prison comedian. But I made an effort to be a good neighbour and a good listener.

Then by chance I fell into the practice of reading and writing letters for prisoners who struggled to read and write – a large group who kept me busy with their requests for help with correspondence which was often on the most intricate subjects imaginable! As one old lag in Belmarsh quipped: "Hey Jonno! Do you realize that with all this letter-writing business of yours, you are making a fantastic impact on the girls of Brixton? They can't believe the improvement in the love letters they are now getting from this nick."

Whatever I was or was not doing for the girls of Brixton, helping my fellow prisoners did wonders for my own morale. I was being useful, serving the community. Try to find your own route to some similar service and your spirits will lift too.

Coming to terms can be a spiritual as well as a practical process. Do you ever pray? Never? Hardly ever? Sometimes? Or perhaps quite often in times of trouble? Surveys suggest that although less than 10 per cent of the population ever go to a church, a mosque, or a place of worship, well over 90 per cent pray at some moment or other. So give it a try. Monks, down the centuries, found that cells can be great places to pray in. The same can be true for prison cells. You don't have to be a godly person to get God's attention.

> You don't have to be a godly person to get God's attention.

Of course, he can tell the difference between sincere and insincere prayers, which brings us back to the importance of not being in denial. You can't con an all-knowing God by claiming you didn't do anything wrong.

On the other hand, God loves a repentant sinner. Jesus told the story of the prodigal son, who asked his father to give him his half of his inheritance. The young man went off to a distant country, where he wasted all his money on booze and women. When he ran out of money all his friends deserted him, and he had to take the worst jobs just to be able to eat. He decided to go back to his father, asking for a job as one of his father's servants. But his father, who had been keeping an eye on the road, rushed out to meet him and welcomed him with open arms. (The full story can be found in Luke 15:11–32.)

This is a picture of what God is like. He will rush out to you, just as he did in the parable of the prodigal son, to the sinner who says, "I'm really sorry. Help me make a fresh start. Please hear my prayers for myself and my family." Even if this sounds improbable or even corny, try starting to pray and stick with it. The old saying "When you're in a hole – stop digging" can be rephrased as, "When you're in a hole – start praying."

Every prisoner who wants to come to terms with both the short-term realities and the long-term hopes for his or her situation needs to find an individual set of ladders out of the depths. Stopping being in denial; engaging helpfully with fellow prisoners; defeating fear; finding hope; and starting to pray are just five potential ways of "coming to terms".

If you try some of them, or all of them, you will get results. Good luck!

EDWARD

Learning the rules of prison life is simple enough. You will soon realize that prison-issue toothpaste is more use as an adhesive than for the purpose indicated on its packaging, which is a discovery worth making sooner rather than later.

More importantly, you will soon get a sense of which prison officers will be more inclined to offer assistance than others. This is valuable, and time-saving.

Getting to grips with the realities of your new situation will take some time, but will come automatically. As you begin to operate more naturally within the limits of the prison regime, life will become a little more comfortable, because you will start to develop a small circle of friends whom you trust.

When you find yourself in prison, the human impulse to be accepted is no less strong than on the outside, even if that "acceptance" is rooted simply in the desire not to stick out. It's a fine line, though: be too placid and you will make yourself vulnerable to being taken advantage of; too much "front" and you'll soon be put in your place one way or another. As you begin to work all these things out, though, and as you develop a routine of sorts, things start to get easier: this is when you begin to "come to terms" with what has happened to you.

No one had expected that I would go to prison. There was a chance, for sure, and I had packed a bag, but as I took a last look at the shocked faces of my friends sat in court, attempted to offer a reassuring half-smile, and was led through the door and down the steps to the cells to be deprived of my tie, belt, and shoelaces, a reality which I had not really allowed myself to properly consider was forcefully being revealed to me.

As the transport van later pulled away, through the darkened window I saw my best friend, a lonely figure standing on the empty pavement outside the court, talking on the phone. As we left him behind a potent mix of shock and fear swept over me. Despite the shouting, banging, and laughing coming from the other four passengers confined to the sweatbox, I felt alone like never before.

That mix of shock and fear carried me through perhaps the first two weeks of my prison experience. But as I settled in and began to get my first letters, the shock and the fear lessened.

The scales tipped at about 8:30 a.m. on a Tuesday morning. I had taken a shower and made a phone call in the half-hour since the cells had been unlocked, and I was leaning against the railings, looking out at the wing, waiting to go to the laundry where I would spend the day trying not to look at stains too closely or think too hard about the various soiled garments and sheets I was processing.

Out of the blue the force of it – the realization of what I faced – hit me physically. I crumpled and began to cry – to weep, really. I was fortunate to be standing next to a "Listener" – a trained and experienced prisoner – who later told me that he had been wondering for a few days when I was going to "go".

He and another Listener whisked me off into a private room and let me ramble on as I tried to express the feelings I had hidden from myself.

Crying is the prisoner's secret shame. Tears betray emotions, and to some men emotions imply an absence of masculinity – a dangerous trait with which to become associated, especially in prison.

But why was I crying – why will you cry, in the privacy of your cell, or publicly and unexpectedly?

The first – and knottiest – reason may be guilt.

It is hard to come to terms with the fact that your actions have been so bad that you have been imprisoned for them. You are, in effect, coming to terms with the fact that the person you thought you knew is an illusion. You used to believe that you wouldn't dream of harming another person. You once thought you would never carelessly and wilfully disregard the welfare of others. You once believed you were one of the good guys. You now know none of that is true. So you cry, because you are forced to examine your own soul, and you find it a darker, more terrifying place than you have ever accepted.

But you will also cry because of your relationships.

Your shaming will have been, to a greater or lesser extent, public, and you will have forced your friends and family to choose, to make a judgment. Do they forgive you? Do they think you are worthy of their continued support? Are they shamed by their association with you? "Did you not *think* about what this would do to the people who love you?" I was asked more than once. Of course, the answer was

The pain of coming to terms with your current situation and your new reality is your journey's first, and hardest, step.

"No". These are the unintended consequences of your actions and they are a heavy burden to carry.

You may also experience an emotion that feels like grief. In a way, it is grief: you are grieving for a life which feels lost to you, a loss felt even more acutely, perhaps, because you did it to yourself.

Your story doesn't end here, though, as much as it might feel like it. The road back is long and bumpy, but it exists. It will be the journey of your life, that much is certain; and for most it is a journey without a map. But one thing is sure. The pain of coming to terms with your current situation and your new reality is your journey's first, and hardest, step. As you take it, do so in the knowledge of all the others who have done so before you, and will do so after you, and in the knowledge of our prayers for you.

Your spirit is stronger than you think

As you settle in to the routine of prison you will begin to look around you more thoughtfully than you might have managed in the early days of your sentence. And as you do so, you will begin to spot – and soon find it very easy to spot – those of your fellow prisoners who have not "come to terms" with their present reality. Fighting against it, resisting it – physically and emotionally – is not only exhausting but actually makes things worse. The more you fight, the worse things get. Your spirit is stronger than you think. Actively work on making peace with your circumstances.

However you seek to achieve this – through prayer, conversation, writing, or any number of other methods – you will likely find this to be the hardest part of your sentence, but it is also, without question, the most important.

Heavenly Father,

As I set out on this frightening journey,

walk alongside me, and grant me the wisdom to see your presence with me always.

Lessen my guilt, comfort me in my grief, and strengthen the bonds between me and those I love.

Your Son Jesus Christ is the way, the truth, and the life.

Give me the strength and courage to follow him, and to come closer to you, loving God.

Amen.

Chapter 3
Chaplains

It may have been a long time since you've come into contact with a priest. Or perhaps it's less than a week since you were sat in church, praying hard that you would be back in that same pew the following week, and not in a prison cell.

Either way, the prison chaplain is the one member of staff you can be sure will make time to listen to you, whatever you're feeling, and whether it has anything to do with God or not.

Their job is not to "convert" you – in fact they are expressly forbidden from attempting to do so – but rather to listen, to counsel, not to judge. And, certainly, to pray for you. As we emphasize elsewhere in this book, prison may be an important moment in your own journey of faith; and if that is the case then the chaplain will be delighted to walk with you for this part of it.

Reflections

JONATHAN

Your prison chaplain should be helpful to you throughout your prison journey, as a friend, spiritual counsellor, confidant, and as a source of advice to you on personal and family issues. So make good use of him or her. I was able to do this throughout my sentence and enjoyed a good relationship with the chaplain in my three different prisons: HMPs Belmarsh, Standford Hill, and Elmley.

Since becoming a prison chaplain in 2018 I have gained a far better understanding of the role, having seen it and experienced it on both sides of the cell door.

The role of a prison chaplain as we understand it was created by the Prisons Act 1952. Every prison is required by law to have a managing chaplain who heads the chaplaincy team. He or she supervises all the other chaplains in the department. Depending on the size of the prison there will be several other chaplains in a variety of faiths or denominations. There is always an Anglican chaplain, a Roman Catholic chaplain, and probably other Christian denomination chaplains such as Orthodox, Methodist, and Pentecostal chaplains. There is always a Muslim chaplain in every prison. Often there is also a Hindu chaplain, a Sikh chaplain, and a Jewish rabbi. In addition, there can be other chaplains from even wider backgrounds. In some prisons the Prison Service employs humanist chaplains, "no faith chaplains", Pagan chaplains, Rastafarian chaplains, Zoroastrian chaplains, and one or two others.

From the above summary it is clear the word "chaplain" is a somewhat elastic term in the Prison Service. Some chaplains do not carry out spiritual or faith-based duties. So what does a chaplain actually do?

Chaplains have certain statutory duties. They are required to see every new prisoner within twenty-four hours of arrival. They should also make daily visits to prisoners in health care units. Chaplains should also make daily visits to the segregation unit to check on each individual prisoner. These checks involve much box ticking and form filling under the present rules. Sometimes they result in conversations that may help the prisoners, or even prevent self-harming or suicide attempts. But quite frequently a chaplain gets rebuffed with negative grunts or even with shouts of "F**k off Pie" ("pie and liquor" equals "vicar" in London prison slang).

Whenever I encounter such hostility I try to respond by playing my trump card: "Hey, I was a prisoner myself once. Would you like to talk?" Often they do, so a conversation starts which can result in shared prayer. I have a calling to pray with prisoners, usually in a one-to-one setting. I listen to their needs, which frequently include the needs of their families, and then we pray together. This form of prayer ministry seems to be well appreciated.

Chaplains conduct services in the chapel, mosque, or interfaith rooms. They can lead Bible studies, prayer groups, or courses such as Alpha or Christianity Explored. They are also mentors, spiritual guides, welfare advisers, bereavement counsellors, and solvers of personal problems. A chaplain needs to have a good heart and to be a good listener.

The multiplicity of chaplaincy functions described above means that chaplains tend to be overworked. They can get overloaded with admin duties. When I was a prisoner at HMP Standford Hill I remember meeting one of the chaplains who looked utterly exhausted. "I've spent the whole evening monitoring international telephone calls," he complained. Such tasks seem far removed from the cure of souls.

Despite the overwork and numerous other problems, most chaplains are dedicated to making life more bearable for the prisoners they serve. Although they carry keys, they rarely deserve the label occasionally applied to them of "screws in dog collars". Chaplains are not there to tell you what to do. They are bridge builders to the gentler side of prison life. They help the milk of human kindness to flow through the wings. For example, they often pass on loving messages from prisoners' families.

> **Remember that chaplains are sinners too.**

In the dark environment of a prison, chaplains can be beacons of light and hope. Inspired by the teachings of their faith they bring compassion inside the prison walls. Remember that chaplains are sinners too. Reach out to them as fellow human beings and they may help you to find, even in tough times, the riches of God's grace.

EDWARD

I could hear Dominic, in the cell next to mine, pacing the floor and stopping occasionally to beat the wall in frustration. Normally I would have complained, but Dominic and I got on well and these weren't normal circumstances.

The gate onto the wing a few metres from our cells clanged open and was then locked shut; footsteps and the jangle of keys approached. Dominic's observation-flap was roughly opened and a voice I didn't recognize said – loudly enough for me to hear – "Hi. I'm the Muslim chaplain. It's a girl!"

"What?! Oh my God. Tell them. Tell them!" replied Dominic.

The chaplain turned and shouted into the wing, "Dominic's wife has had a girl!"

There was a second or two of silence, presumably as three floors of men hauled themselves off their beds. Then they proceeded to show their appreciation and congratulations in that uniquely prison-based fashion: repeatedly kicking their metal cell doors as hard as possible. The noise was deafening and, weirdly, heart-warming.

This was probably not how Dominic had expected to hear the news of his daughter's birth; and in the course of a number of conversations we had discussed the sense of guilt and shame he felt for having got himself sent to prison leaving a pregnant wife at home, alone, to cope with their toddler. But she had stuck with him, and her presence in the visits hall, particularly in the couple of weeks before the chaplain's shouted news, was easy to spot. Later Dominic would face the difficult situation of meeting his new child for the first time in the course of a regular visit, in front of a hall full of perhaps 400 other people.

Prison rules about who can be unlocked, when, and for what reason are complex. Being informed of the birth of a child through a locked door seems, in hindsight, almost cruel. But from Dominic's pacing and wall-beating I think he was just pleased to know, and to be sure that his wife was well. Delivering good news happens less often for chaplains than delivering bad, and although I'd like to think that bad news is given in a more sensitive way, it is invariably to the chaplains – of whatever faith or denomination: Dominic was not a Muslim – that this task falls.

The prison chaplain occupies a distinct and unique position in the prison community. Chaplains do not neatly fit into that two-part system of identification on which prisons operate: us or them. Their role is to minister to prisoners and staff without taking sides, and without breaking confidences. They are often called upon to do the "touchy-feely stuff" – both good and bad – and from the outside it can often seem as if the chaplaincy team simply spend their days racing from one pastoral crisis to another. Prisons are not short of pastoral crises.

As you arrive from court to your first prison, you will be asked your religion. There are any number of reasons why, during the course of your processing (hardly a stress-free experience), you might feel like ticking the "no religion" box. Perhaps, like me, your feelings about your god and your faith are highly mixed in light of the day's events; perhaps you worry whether labelling yourself

Perhaps you feel that, because faith hasn't played a particularly large part in your life until now, it would be dishonest to throw yourself on God's mercy.

as a paid-up member of the God-squad is wise; or perhaps you feel that, because faith hasn't played a particularly large part in your life until now, it would be dishonest to throw yourself on God's mercy when things get tough.

Put aside that last observation for the moment (though remember the story about the prodigal son). If in doubt, tick the box. And if in doubt as to which box to tick, tick "Church of England". The worst that will happen as a result of this is that you'll get a visit from the CofE chaplain in your first couple of days. They will not expect nor pressure

35

you to talk about faith. They will be concerned with your welfare and they will be a compassionate and reassuring presence as you settle in to your new environment. If you want to talk about religious stuff then they will be delighted to do so, but this conversation will be started only by you.

Being a prison chaplain is a specific and unusual calling. Jonathan's journey to prison ministry is a particularly clear example of God using our lives and our experience for good – even when we think we've screwed up beyond redemption. But every prison chaplain has a reason for ministering in prison, and one thing is sure: it's not an easy environment in which to wear the dog-collar. As a visible symbol of God and religion, chaplains receive the anger which is really directed upwards; and they sit with people who are at their lowest ebb, day after day. They may be familiar with this, but that doesn't mean they are indifferent to it. To offer someone true and effective care involves giving up a little piece of one's own self – making oneself a little bit vulnerable in order to establish trust.

The chaplain does this day after day, willingly and gladly. But as they pray for you, pray for them too. If you're new to prayer, or are finding it particularly difficult in your new circumstances, then simply saying "thank you" to God for your prison chaplains is a pretty good place to start.

There to listen, to talk, and to pray

The Church of England doesn't talk much about its prison chaplains. Society doesn't like thinking about its prisons, and this sometimes seems to extend to pews and pulpits. And that doesn't make sense, because the chaplains who minister to those who live and work in our prisons are living out the gospel in a self-giving way which ought to be recognized, supported, celebrated, and imitated by the rest of us.

In the days after it was announced that one of the authors of this book was to become a prison chaplain, the other author read an article on the website of a national newspaper recounting this new deacon's nineteen-year, third-of-a-mile journey

The chaplains who minister to those who live and work in our prisons are living out the gospel in a self-giving way.

from the Old Bailey to St Paul's Cathedral. The following remark in the comments section stood out: "I respect him finding God and wanting to help other people, but why does he have to seek *status* like this?"

The person who made that comment completely failed to grasp the role of the priest. The chaplains ministering to you in prison are not interested in *status*, their own or yours. Perhaps that's part of the reason those on the outside don't pay them much attention. They are not interested in the prison hierarchy, nor in making moral judgments about the circumstances and actions which have led you to this point. They are there to listen, to talk, and to pray.

The famous hymn "What a Friend we Have in Jesus" asks:

Are we weak and heavy-laden,
Cumbered with a load of care?
Precious Saviour, still our refuge –
Take it to the Lord in prayer.

Taking it to the Lord in prayer is good advice, especially when we find it difficult to say what exactly that "it" is. Presenting ourselves as we are – scared, confused, angry – is enough. But if, beneath it all, all that is left is a cry for help, don't discount the possibility that the chaplain knocking on your cell door might be the beginning of God's answer.

Lord God Almighty,

You have sent your servants into this place to minister to me and those with whom I live.

Give them strength as they give a little more of themselves each day; and afford me the courage gladly to clasp their outstretched hand of friendship.

Amen.

Chapter 4
Chapel Life

You may not have spent much time in church. Most people used to have some connection with a church, but churchgoing is not as common as it used to be (though cathedrals are getting more and more popular).

However, you have probably noticed the chaplaincies and chapels that have sprung up in new places. Almost every hospital has a chaplain and a chapel. So do airports, many shopping centres, schools – and, of course, prisons.

The former Archbishop of Canterbury, Rowan Williams, pointed out that these chapels and chaplaincies serve people who are "living away from their natural support structures" – an accurate description of prison. Most of us rely upon natural support structures, such as our families and familiar places, for our sense of identity. But when we are away from our families, in a strange place, it is often then that God chooses to speak to us.

There is a tradition in Christianity called Celtic spirituality. One of the important ideas in Celtic spirituality is that of "thin places", where the distance between heaven and earth – between us and God – seems, somehow, smaller than usual. In such places, God can seem more real. A "thin place" may be somewhere particularly beautiful, or peaceful, or astonishing, but not always. Prison can also be a "thin place".

It may surprise you, but the worshipping life of the chapel in your prison will be amongst the most vibrant and enthusiastic you will ever experience. You will find joy there unlike anywhere else behind prison walls.

At your prison chapel you will also probably discover despair more profound than can possibly be imagined.

This is where God dwells: where he is praised, where he is pleaded with, and where he is cursed. This is a true "thin place", where Christ makes himself known in the breaking of the bread, in the singing of songs, in the praying of prayers. Your prison chapel is a place where you can take yourself, and God, more seriously.

For where two or three are gathered in my name,
there am I among them.
(Matthew 18:20, ESV)

Reflections

JONATHAN

"Anyone wanting to go to chapel on Sunday must book in with the wing office on Thursday evening," said the announcement over the tannoy. "Passes will then be issued on a first-come, first-served basis."

You may need to plan ahead to get to the chapel in your prison. That's not a bad thing, as it allows you time to think about what you are doing there.

Although a prison chapel should in theory be the House of God, in practice it usually doubles up as a venue for a whole range of ordinary activities. Because space is often short in prison, chapels are frequently used for film showings, yoga classes, AA meetings, anger-management classes, staff briefings, management meetings, and many other purposes.

Despite these pressures, services in prison chapels are usually well run by the chaplains, chapel volunteers, musicians, staff, and prisoners who attend the Sunday services. There will also be other spiritual events such as Bible study groups, prayer fellowship meetings, or Alpha courses. It may take a little perseverance to get to your chapel on a regular basis, but keep trying. You will find that the opportunities it offers can be an important resource as you try to turn your prison journey into a spiritual journey.

When I was moved to a D-Cat open prison, access to chapel became much easier. So I made a point of attending the daily service of Morning Prayer at 8:30 a.m. I found that when I began each day by reading aloud a psalm, a passage from the Bible, and sharing some communal prayers with the chaplain and a handful of fellow inmates, it created a sense of peace within me which usually lasted for the rest of the day.

Chapel orderlies, in my experience, can be angels disguised in prison uniform. Their kindness and helpfulness can shine like a beacon of light in the gloom of jail tensions. Confide in them and in your chaplains too. The latter are often rushed off their feet by administrative chores but they should always make time for pastoral care and careful listening.

For me the best part of chapel life was sharing prayers and worship with my fellow prisoners. On one Sunday service I found myself standing alongside a grizzled old lag who was coming toward the end of his umpteenth sentence for multiple burglaries and robberies. We were singing "Through All the Changing Scenes of Life" when all of a sudden this tough muscular figure broke down in floods of tears.

As he wept, I put an arm around his shoulder and enquired sympathetically: "Have you had a knock-back, Charlie? Some bad news from home?"

"No – I'm crying because I'm so happy," he explained. "I've been doing literacy classes. This is the first time in me life that I can read the bleedin' words and I am beginning to see what God's really about."

The chapel is a sacred space where you can hear God whispering to you, and perhaps telling you what he can do for those who reach out for him in penitence and prayer.

During my sentence I became drawn into a circle of praying men who included a blagger (an armed robber), a dipper (a pickpocket), a kiter (fraudster), two lifers (murderers), and a blower (safe cracksman). This unusual gathering met nightly. The group made a profound impact on me and helped my growing relationship with Jesus Christ. Only in a prison chapel could I have come to love such neighbours and learn from them about the generosity of God's grace to us sinners.

Only in a prison chapel could I have come to love such neighbours.

EDWARD

The chapels of Her Majesty's Prisons are as different from one another as the churches we walk past each day in the outside world.

Step into the chapel of HMP Wormwood Scrubs and you will be greeted by stained glass, a beautifully tiled floor, and a series of panels painted by prisoners. The chapel of, say, HMP High Down, on the other hand, is just a large room with bars at the windows, low ceilings, and a rather odd altar. A church is not the building, though, and so in many ways the architecture doesn't matter. Whatever it looks like, for many prisoners the chapel is the beating heart of the prison, and the services and Bible study groups each week provide a welcome routine.

After the first two Sundays I asked if I could switch from the Anglican services to the Roman Catholic. I'm not a Catholic, but I was used to attending Mass regularly, and it is a big part of my spiritual life. The Anglicans held Mass just once a month, while the Roman Catholics held Mass every week. Strictly speaking it was against the rules for the Catholic chaplain to give me communion, but he did so anyway. It meant a lot to me.

As with all other aspects of prison life, though, chapel has its moments of absurdity. The second – and final – Anglican service of my sentence was the scene of an "is this really happening?" moment as the chaplain announced that we would now sing "If I Were a Butterfly" – a song which I thought I knew, but couldn't quite remember from where. The Lord in his great mercy had allowed me to forget of its existence until this moment; but by the time a chapel full of burly, still relatively intimidating, blokes arrived at the line

I had last heard some decades earlier in a primary-school assembly, "And if I were a fuzzy-wuzzy bear, I'd thank you, Lord, for my fuzzy-wuzzy hair," not unwelcome tears of laughter were rolling down my cheeks.

The chapel is also a source of much free stuff for those who attend, from Bibles to magazines to rosaries. A4-sized posters of Jesus, Mary, and a host of saints were handed out at Mass, and I often accepted them, mainly out of a desire to brighten up my boring cell. I didn't take them all that seriously.

However, one day I left my cell, which was fast taking on the appearance of a giftshop at Lourdes, and went to retrieve a book I had lent to a middle-aged Polish man with whom I attended chapel. As I entered his cell, I glimpsed through clouds of cigarette-smoke one of the same pictures of the Sacred Heart which adorned my own. My friend, though, had crafted from matchsticks and glue the most spectacular and ornate frame in which the picture now sat; a picture which was the centrepiece of the small space, and which he contemplated each day as he prayed. I was impressed, moved, and ashamed.

A small diary – which I still possess – was given to me the day after my arrival in prison, by one of the Free Church chaplains. Each day had a verse from the Bible, and as I wrote (in capitals, presumably for dramatic effect) "SENTENCED" on the previous day's line, my eye was drawn to its first verse, John 1:1: "In the beginning was the Word, and the Word was with God, and the Word was God" (NIV).

This is no easy "it'll all be all right" verse. It rewards the kind of deep, prolonged contemplation for which prison provides plenty of time.

Prison is a place where time and space are tightly controlled. In prison time passes painfully slowly, while outside life is rushing ahead. The sentence you are serving represents the end of one life, and life after prison can seem like a dream. I found that this verse, which goes far beyond our mortal understanding of God, of time, and of order, was deeply comforting. It is a verse familiar to a wider audience than regular church- or chapel-goers, as it forms the high point of the liturgy of Nine Lessons and Carols, a service which draws through the doors of the parish church those who would normally steer clear, and which many millions listen to or watch when it is broadcast on Christmas Eve from King's College, Cambridge.

Each year, as I watch or listen to this service, the reading of this verse is a bittersweet moment, but perhaps that's no bad thing. For as the gospel passage continues, "And the light shineth in darkness; and the darkness comprehended it not" (John 1:5, KJV). Prisons are society's dark places, but it is in the darkest corners of our world that the light – Christ, Light of the World – shines most brightly.

Those who have sat in a prison cell know better than most the burning intensity of that light, whether we fully comprehend it, or not.

Prisons are society's dark places, but it is in the darkest corners of our world that the light – Christ, Light of the World – shines most brightly.

Enjoy the fellowship

To begin with, attending chapel will be unfamiliar. Perhaps moving off the wing and being in a room with a large number of new people will be intimidating. Perhaps you're not a regular churchgoer on the outside and you are concerned that you won't know what to do and when.

Well, you couldn't have picked a better place to try churchgoing. Services in prison certainly aren't stiff or formal. You will quickly find that, amongst the noise and the clamour, the chapel is a place of strong faith and you can't help but be swept along. For that hour or so each week, enjoy the fellowship and rejoice in the knowledge that, just for a while, the prison walls crumble away and you are joining with millions of other Christians around the world in singing hymns of praise to God.

> **Lord God,**
>
> **Grant me the strength and the bravery
> to open myself to you;**
>
> **open my ears that I may listen for your still small
> voice of calm amongst the noise of the prison,**
>
> **free my tongue to speak your word,
> sing your praise, and share your gospel,**
>
> **and help me see those most in need
> of love and compassion.**
>
> **Through Christ, our strength and our redeemer,**
>
> **Amen.**

Chapter 5
Prison Officers

Say "prison officer" to the man or woman on the street, and the chances are that you can predict what they are thinking. Popular culture has a lot to answer for.

Anyone who's been inside a prison, however, will know that the ranks of prison officers are at least as diverse (in some respects) as the prisoners for whom they are responsible. Certainly you will meet a lot of military veterans; but that will be true for prisoners, too. There will be more than double the number of men than women, and the likelihood is that, increasingly, prisoners will notice that their officers are getting younger. This will get more noticeable as the proportion of elderly prisoners increases.

There is no "typical prison officer" – just as there is no "typical prisoner" – particularly in the eyes of God.

The point is, though, that there is no "typical prison officer" – just as there is no "typical prisoner" – particularly in the eyes of God. The individual stories of those who find themselves locking the doors are every bit as interesting and varied as the stories of those who are locked up.

Reflections

JONATHAN

Prison officers are not your enemies.

Because they are in authority, they will never become your friends on an equal basis. But they share a common goal with you. It is to make the prison environment safe, fair, decent, and compassionate, in an atmosphere where mutual respect flourishes. Help your officers to achieve this goal and you will become happier and more spiritually fulfilled yourself.

While I was serving my eighteen-month sentence for perjury I gradually came to admire most of the prison officers I encountered. But I started out on my prison journey believing that cons and screws were two hostile tribes, often at war with each other.

Although this is generally fiction, it is not always untrue. In the year this book was written there were over 10,000 assaults in the UK upon prison staff by inmates – nearly 4,000 of them serious attacks. Even if these figures decline, as they probably will because of the steadily increasing recruitment of new officers, violent attacks by a small minority of inmates upon officers will remain a fact of prison life.

Try looking at this problem from the prison officers' point of view. They are ordinary human beings too, with ordinary lives at home. The last thing they want to do is to get injured in a punch-up with an inmate who may be high on drugs, mentally unstable, or boiling over with anger. Because prisons are pressure cookers in which irrational acts of violence occur too often, prison officers are trained to be handy in a fight if one starts. But far more of their training is devoted to preventing the conditions and situations in which anger becomes rage.

On my first day of duty as a prison chaplain in HMP Pentonville in July 2018, I learned at the governor's management meeting that only 61 officers were going to be on duty due to staff shortages and summer holidays. How on earth, I wondered, were 61 officers supposed to control over 1,300 prisoners? The answer is by the chemistry of consent. Prison officers don't just do a job. Only in the tabloids are they mere jailers and turnkeys.

Those of us who see prison officers at work in this community know that they have a range of skills which run from being amateur psychiatrists to father figures, to humourists, to encouragers, to problem solvers. They are also good at following an old biblical proverb – "A gentle answer turns anger away" (Proverbs 15:1, NIRV) – which works surprisingly often.

They have a range of skills which run from being amateur psychiatrists to father figures, to humourists, to encouragers, to problem solvers.

Prison officers are often remarkable people. I will always remember my personal officer, Joe Rook at HMP Standford Hill, who was an inspirational figure of kindness, humour, and robust common sense. I also remember, on my last night as a prisoner in HMP Elmley, how an unknown officer, who gave his name simply as "Mr Smith", knocked on my cell door after midnight and whispered through the observation panel:

"I know you're being released tomorrow and as your brother in Christ I wanted to send you away with a prayer."

So Prison Officer Smith and Prisoner CB9298 Aitken whispered a prayer or two together through the grill of the cell door. This was all but impossible in the prison culture; but with God all things are possible. I shall always remember that holy moment which told me then, and tells me now, that prison officers can be good and remarkable people.

EDWARD

Prisons are full of people; and places full of people are full of relationships: prisoner–prisoner; prisoner–staff; staff–staff. At the best of times and in the best of places, the web of relationships between a group of people is going to be complicated. Because prison officers have a lot of power, the relationships are more complicated still.

For most new arrivals in prisons, it's probably been a while – or perhaps it's *hopefully* been a while – since you had to do what you were told, just because the other person is in charge. It will be easier for you if you learn quickly that, in prison, this will often be the only explanation you get for a particular request. You will quickly discover that it isn't smart to ask for reasons.

I am not suggesting you make yourself a doormat, but it is wise to pick your battles. In prison, you will have to obey a host of instructions which sometimes don't make sense. The fact that an order is difficult to grasp doesn't mean the order is stupid. But sometimes you will not be able to see the point of a command, and when that happens you need to learn to control your frustration. Remember that, most of the time, the person doing the asking will not be trying to make your life difficult. They may even be equally frustrated!

One day, when you come to think back on your time in prison, you will realize that prison officers occupy the same space in your memory as schoolteachers: you will remember the very best and the very worst. The vast majority – those who were "fine" – will slowly fade away from your mind, until all that are left of the hundreds of officers you will come across during your time in prison will be the unusual ones, the angels and the demons; the saints and the sinners.

In many ways, that is a shame, because it is these "fine" prison officers who keep the wheels turning: they may not stand out, but they want a calm, safe, productive environment in which to do their jobs, and they want to go home to their families without sporting the scars – physical and mental – which they can easily suffer when that workplace ceases to be calm, safe, and productive.

There will be a few you might want to forget, but can't. As with any place where there are lots of people, there will be a few bad apples. As a rule, these officers are no more than generally unpleasant or unfair. All the same, such injustices, however slight, will be amplified in prison, so it can take a real effort to rise above them.

Most of the time, it's worth it to stay calm. An officer may be trying to wind you up. If you respond in anger, you may find yourself being disciplined, which can be unpleasant. Turning the other cheek (Matthew 5:39) is hard; and it will sometimes be necessary to respond sharply – that is a judgment you will have to make. But for the low-level stuff, turning the other cheek is the best thing you can do. You will prove yourself to not be worth the effort of provoking, and your life will be quieter and easier as a result. And when you've calmed down – when the anger and resentment have subsided – pray for your officers. Pray for those with whom you don't see eye to eye;

For the low-level stuff, turning the other cheek is the best thing you can do. You will prove yourself to not be worth the effort of provoking.

follow the advice of Jesus just a few verses later and "...pray for those who persecute you" (Matthew 5:44, NIV).

Pray also for the many officers who will go out of their way for you. Many of them feel called to work in prison. A comment I have heard over and over again from officers, both in prison and in conversations since I was released, runs along the lines of, "It could be my son, my brother, my father who goes to prison. I know how I'd want them treated." This basic humanity should not be exceptional and, indeed, usually isn't. But the fact that those officers, working in a flawed system where they see the same faces returning, keep hold of hope, means that you can too. Prison officers are – by and large – *good* people who want the best for you, and for themselves. Treat them with the humanity and decency you would like in return and you won't go far wrong. They are, for better or worse, your neighbours; and Jesus was clear about what he expects of us in relation to our neighbours:

One of them, an expert in the law, tested him with this question: "Teacher, which is the greatest commandment in the Law?" Jesus replied: "'Love the Lord your God with all your heart and with all your soul and with all your mind.' This is the first and greatest commandment. And the second is like it: 'Love your neighbour as yourself.' All the Law and the Prophets hang on these two commandments." (Matthew 22:35–40, NIV)

Community is often a challenge

Prison is a community, and living in community is often a challenge. Monks know this; so do prisoners. It's even more of a challenge when some of the people in the community have far more power than others, and it's particularly a problem if those who have little power used to have a lot.

Unquestionably, this will be a difficult adjustment. But it is one worth making sooner rather than later. You want your time in prison to be calm, safe, and productive, and so do prison officers. Treat them as your enemy and the consequences for your time inside will not be happy. Be civil and helpful – without licking anyone's boots – and things will be a lot easier. But above all, bring them before God – *pray* for them. A good few of them will be doing the same for you.

You want your time in prison to be calm, safe, and productive, and so do prison officers.

Loving God,

I bring the officers and staff
of my prison before you;

Care for them, protect them, and fill them
with your compassion and love.

Foster strong and respectful relationships
between officers and prisoners,

that our community might be a safe, caring,
and purposeful environment.

Through your Son, our saviour, Jesus Christ,

Amen.

Chapter 6
Drugs in Prison, and Other Temptations

Prisons are places to which you get sent if you break the rules.

They exist, depending on your point of view, either to punish and scare you out of doing so again, or to rehabilitate you to the same end.

But there are lots of rules in prison and, let's be honest, lots of people in prison who aren't particularly keen on keeping them. Perhaps the most destructive type of rule-breaking relates to drugs. Media headlines of prisons being "awash" with illegal substances aren't far off the mark. On the morning this chapter was written, a report was published which

Although prison may be one of the easiest places to get hold of drugs, it is also the place where you can get the right kind of help to quit.

claimed that one in seven prisoners become addicted to some form of drug during their sentence. It's hard to forgive those who organize the smuggling of drugs into prisons for financial gain, particularly when you have seen first-hand the destruction these substances cause in people's lives.

But alongside the misery and destruction sit organizations and individuals whose mission it is to help those who struggle with addiction. Although prison may be one of the easiest places to get hold of drugs, it is also the place where you can get the right kind of help to quit. Prison will offer you serious temptation, but also serious opportunity. What leads to one instead of the other? Some would say only one thing: you. And true enough, getting clean, or resisting the temptation to take a substance which seems to wipe out some of your sentence, requires you to be strong.

But you are not alone. Drugs are one of the true evils of contemporary life. But with Christ at your side, just as he is in every other facet of prison life, those evils can be faced down and beaten.

Reflections

JONATHAN

On my first weekend as a prisoner in HMP Belmarsh I saw so many of my fellow cons "clucking" (lurching unsteadily around making hen-like noises) that I thought I was in some drug den rather than an English jail.

"How on earth do they get hold of their drugs?" I asked my cell neighbour.

"Bottling it, panelling, and gumming it," was the reply, which left me none the wiser. Eventually, I had these terms translated into, "sticking it up the anus", "smuggling it inside a parcel", and "getting your wife/girlfriend to hold it in her mouth and then pass it over in a goodbye kiss at the end of the visit".

Drugs flow like a river through most prisons. Halting the flow would be hugely expensive in terms of staff overtime or new technology. The Prison Service is getting better at fighting its drug battles but is nowhere near winning this war. So drug abuse is a fact of life in most prisons. You will not have to work hard to be led into drug temptation as an inmate. Pushers are everywhere. The outside barons of the drug trade heavily subsidize the prices for their prison customers. Payments are enforced by violence on the inside or by equally brutal debt collections after you get out. Frequently wives and families get trapped into this cycle by "visits from the crack bailiffs" as they are called. It is a messy, nasty business.

"Lead us not into temptation" (Luke 11:4, NIV) says the prayer Jesus taught us. Easier said than done if you become hooked while doing your sentence.

But ladders are available for climbing out of the living hell of addiction. Because of the size of the problem, every prison has drug counsellors, drug-free substance abuse wings, and courses provided by expert charities in this field such as the Forward Trust. It is wise to sign on for them early.

The long-established Narcotics Anonymous (NA) and Alcoholics Anonymous (AA) "Twelve Step" courses tend to advise, "You may not be able to get beyond Step Number 10 by your own will power. You may need the help of a higher power." What does this mean? Whose power are these courses referring to? In today's multifaith, multicultural society the answer gets blurred and vague. But many decades ago, when AA started up, its Christian founders knew exactly what they were describing: God's power.

The healing power that Jesus offered to all sinners can be accessed through prayer and perseverance. I have seen this work so many times that I totally believe in it. But it is not a road offering swift solutions. We all have weak wills, and the temptations offered by drugs are strong. You can get clean by training, discipline, and willpower. But

> **The healing power that Jesus offered to all sinners can be accessed through prayer and perseverance.**

in my observation recovery works faster and deeper, and lasts longer, when strengthened by the power of prayer and belief in a loving God.

"Forgive us our sins" (Luke 11:4, NIV). Alas, most of us have far too many. But gradually we can conquer them, and do so more successfully, if we are praying to a forgiving Father in heaven.

Because prison is an artificial environment its temptations are artificial too. Pornography is a poor substitute for a loving human relationship with the partner of your dreams. Spice, crack, or coke are more dangerous and even more unsatisfying. If you go through the list of your private temptations with brutal honesty, what may dawn on you is that the way to clean up your own act starts within the deepest spiritual corner of your heart, which is called the soul.

In the struggle to get free of drugs, it really helps to have someone you can talk to. Cellmates occasionally become soulmates. Or you might find a soulmate by going to chapel and joining a prayer group. This did wonders for me when I was wrestling with my own temptations. Life starts to feel different when you are starting to follow the two greatest commandments of Jesus: love God, and love your neighbour.

Try reaching out to a neighbour on your wing. Be bold and make a friend of the most unlikely and unlovable character you can find. You may help him a lot, and in the process you may help yourself even more. By starting to obey God and by listening and praying to him, you will leap forward on your journey toward beating your temptations and enjoying a better life.

EDWARD

"The devil finds work for idle hands," your grandmother may once have told you.

The potential for idleness in prison is vast, and if you allow yourself to sink into idleness you can get into all kinds of drug-related trouble. Smuggling, selling, buying, and taking drugs are, without question, the most destructive, misery-inducing illicit activities that take place in our prisons.

The attraction of drugs is many-layered. Some enter prison with drug habits. A depressing number acquire a drug habit while in prison. Some simply use drugs because

> **Smuggling, selling, buying, and taking drugs are, without question, the most destructive, misery-inducing illicit activities that take place in our prisons.**

they are the most effective way of speeding up a sentence, or of ensuring that a good portion of it passes the individual by without their knowledge. This last observation is particularly true of the "new psychoactive substances" such as spice which render the taker zombie-like. These can seem like the only way to escape from an unbearable reality.

The lengths to which some go to bring drugs into prison are truly shocking, especially when you consider that your loved ones risk being sent to prison themselves for smuggling in drugs.

People take drugs for different reasons, and the responses need to vary too. There is a place for punishment. Those who exploit others, and who organize and facilitate the smuggling operations which keep prisons supplied with drugs, really need to be stopped. But punishment is entirely counterproductive for those people who are at the bottom of the chain, working themselves into enormous debts and physical danger by trying to feed their habit, wherever it was acquired. Substance misuse services are standard parts of healthcare provision in prisons, and there are many organizations doing superb work with those who have addiction problems.

The chances are that, at some point during your sentence, you will become aware of the presence of drugs around you. It may even be that, as happened to me, you are seen as the sort of prisoner unlikely to arouse suspicion, so are asked to keep "something" in your cell for a while in return for a healthy payment. Needless to say: don't. But what should your reaction be to that sort of request? Say "no" and turn a blind eye? Report the person who asked to an officer? It's a difficult decision. Being seen as a "grass" is extremely uncomfortable, not to say dangerous, and may have a number of consequences for you. You may even have to be moved to another prison for your own safety. If this happens to you it's difficult not to feel that you are being punished for doing the right thing. Doing nothing, though, cannot be *morally* the right thing, can it? Ultimately, it is your decision: very few would condemn you for turning a blind eye. If you reported such an occurrence, you would certainly be braver than me, and would have my admiration. When I faced this test myself, I stayed silent.

Drugs aside, why break the rules? For Christians, transgression is almost as old as the world itself: temptation presented itself to Eve, and then to Adam, and they – we – without so much as a backwards glance, gave in. One rule decreed by God: one rule immediately broken. It is, usually, the promise of something better – thrilling, exciting, rewarding, pleasurable – that elicits the breaking of rules, as with Adam and Eve; but sometimes it is the *meaning* of the act of breaking the rule which is the end in itself.

Although the first motivation is often the reason people find themselves in prison, the second is perhaps more common once they're there, and lies at the heart of the sort of rule-breaking which is entirely futile; frustratingly petty. As a prisoner you are at the bottom of the heap, and it's tempting to lash out against your situation, particularly if you feel hard done by.

You will very quickly become familiar with those of your fellow prisoners who fight this kind of war against the system, frequently committing relatively minor offences, then citing the absurdity of the rule as a reason for breaking it, or claiming that it treats them as children (which it often does). Breaking the rule then becomes a way of reasserting their adulthood, masculinity, or sense of control. Sometimes, it can be the only way that individual can find to express their rage – a rage which is often less directed at "the system" than it might at first appear and rather more at themselves. It's worth pausing and asking yourself why they might be behaving as they are.

If you should feel tempted to break rules yourself; if you should start to feel that a little disobedience might just give you the sense of control which is often lacking in prison, or might be a good outlet for your annoyance and anger at the petty rules you are being obliged to follow, then have a look at this advice from the letter of James:

> *So then, submit yourselves to God. Resist the Devil, and he will run away from you. (James 4:7, GNB)*

> *My friends, consider yourselves fortunate when all kinds of trials come your way, for you know that when your faith succeeds in facing such trials, the result is the ability to endure. Make sure that your endurance carries you all the way without failing, so that you may be perfect and complete, lacking nothing. (James 1:2–4, GNB)*

This time is different

At some point during your sentence, then, it is almost inevitable that you will become aware of the presence of drugs. It is not an exaggeration to say that how you respond is a future-altering, life-defining decision. Steering clear is easier said than done; but it is the only course of action which we – we who have been there – can recommend. We don't condemn those who get caught in the vicious, destructive spirals of substance abuse, crime, and misery. But remember, it may well have been just this kind of behaviour which landed you in prison in the first place.

Fundamentally, the decision to avoid the more destructive temptations of prison life is an individual's alone. But you will almost certainly reach that decision – whether simply to avoid these temptations in the first place, or whether to seek treatment for addiction, for example – only with the help and support of others.

Here is something you can do. You can be part of that support for your fellow prisoners, whether through casual conversations or, crucially, through prayer. The effects of the "drug epidemic" in our prisons are there for all to see. The misery drugs cause will live long in the memories of those who spend time in prison. Yet good work is being done to relieve the suffering caused by drug and alcohol abuse, by mutual-aid groups and groups like NA and AA. Try to encourage the determination of those whose lives have teetered on the edge of destruction but who have decided that *this time is different*.

It is here, in the courage and honesty of such groups, that you will find that quality which is often buried deep beneath the routines of daily prison life: hope. Hope is sometimes in short supply, but do what you can to nurture and encourage it.

Pray for all those caught in the grip of drugs and other temptations.

Pray for all those caught in the grip of drugs and other temptations; pray for those who see a light, however dim, at the end of their tunnel of misery; and pray for those working to guide individuals toward that light of recovery.

Lord God,

Ever since Adam and Eve gave in to temptation in the Garden of Eden, we have gone out of our way to do things which cause harm to ourselves and to others.

Help me to resist the temptations presented to me in here; strengthen those whose resolve is crumbling; and encourage those who are trying to fix their gaze on the light of recovery.

Thank you for those whose lives are spent in the service of those trapped by addiction: they are doing your work, unrecognized and uncelebrated, saving lives each and every day.

Amen.

Chapter 7
Keeping in Touch with the Outside World

There remains – or perhaps, given our technologically advancing world, there is increasingly – something special about receiving a letter. Not the sort of letter which, from the layout or colour of the type, one can sense contains a demand for some sort of payment, but the sort with a handwritten address – with the promise of contents filled with meaning. Perhaps that content will be serious – the imparting of important news – or perhaps it will simply exist for no reason other than the writer thought of you, and wanted you to think of them.

Letters are not, of course, the only method by which you will be able to keep in touch with the outside world during your sentence, but because other methods are expensive, letters will almost certainly be the main source of communication. And apart from visits, there are very few moments in prison as joyful as the telltale scrape of paper on concrete as a letter is pushed through the gap between your cell door and the floor.

It can be enormously tempting, especially in the early days of your sentence, to erect emotional and communication barriers between you and the rest of the world which mirror the walls and barbed wire surrounding you. But you need to stay in contact with your friends and family. Both of us want to underline the obvious and considerable benefits of not putting up barriers. Try to find the courage to pick up the phone, or write a letter.

> **Try to find the courage to pick up the phone, or write a letter.**

There's something else you can do. We both met many people in prison who, for reasons of nationality or education, found it hard to communicate in writing, and couldn't afford telephone calls. If you are able and willing, lending these people your skills is an easy way of improving their life in prison, and gives you a chance to feel useful again. It is also, without question, the godly thing to do.

Reflections

JONATHAN

If you make a real effort to keep in touch with the outside world during your sentence you will have a happier prison journey, and better chances of going straight after your release.

But it isn't easy to keep in touch. You may feel too down and depressed to make the effort. You may find that writing letters by hand can be a struggle in an age when sending emails is the norm for almost everyone else – except prisoners. You will find it frustrating to make phone calls from prison, battling against long queues, shortage of money on your phonecard, and "number engaged" signals when you do reach the handset. During my sentence I had huge problems with all the above. Three of my nearest and dearest family members were living or studying overseas, so they were horribly expensive to call.

Because of what I used to do, I received a huge postbag of letters each day, between forty and ninety, from both well-wishers and ill-wishers. There weren't many ill-wishers, but still enough to cause pain and discomfort. As the vast majority of my letter writers were kindly souls, I made a great effort to reply to them even if only with a few words on a postcard. I once read that Lord Curzon, when Viceroy of India, managed to write 100 letters every day even when carrying out his official duties. I thought I could make the effort to send out thirty to forty postcards or short letters each day while banged up for up to sixteen hours in a prison cell – and I did.

That effort was well worthwhile both as an antidote to boredom and as a boost to my low morale. I was amazed to discover how many people actually cared enough to express their kind and often prayerful good wishes to Prisoner CB9298 Aitken. So perhaps a good rule about keeping in touch with the outside world is to answer all incoming messages and letters promptly.

Rule number two is to write first. Don't wait for people to contact you. There are several people in your life – friends, relatives, and those who have shown you kindness – who will be glad to hear from you, even though they have not communicated with you. So write to them off your own bat! They may well be fascinated by what you have to tell them about your life in prison. They will certainly be touched that you have taken the trouble to make contact with them.

You might also consider writing to those you have hurt by your actions. I wrote several such letters to people I felt

I had let down badly by the lies which ultimately led to my conviction for perjury. They ranged from cabinet ministers, MPs, senior civil servants, and constituents, to cleaning ladies who had lost their jobs as a result of my bankruptcy and fall from grace. One responded rudely, and a few ignored my letters, but most took the trouble to reply graciously. All your correspondents will be interested by what you have to say about your journey as a prisoner, especially if you include a few touches of humour. They will also be reassured to know that you are coping rather than collapsing.

Some of your correspondents may respond with words to the effect of: "Do come and have a drink after you get out." If so, seize your opportunity to keep in touch with them, and write back. Staying in communication with the outside world is a good way to build bridges with that world after the day of your release. You never know who may be helpful to you when you go through the difficult process of re-entry into the world of freedom. So, follow the advice of Dr Samuel Johnson to "keep your friendships in good repair". If you come out of the prison gate with a list of friends and correspondents with whom you have stayed in touch, you will be rich in opportunities to rebuild relationships and perhaps even get a helping hand with an introduction to a job opportunity. Who knows? One fact of life which is well known is that

> **Staying in communication with the outside world is a good way to build bridges with that world after the day of your release.**

a silent prisoner quickly becomes a forgotten prisoner. So be a communicator!

There are many ways of communicating other than writing letters. Postcards, birthday cards, and Christmas cards are good ways of staying in touch. Time is on your side when it comes to writing them!

For those who do not feel up to writing letters or cards there are other ways to communicate. For example, there is a Prison Service Regulation, introduced in the 1980s by the then Home Secretary Kenneth Baker, which permits a prisoner to send out tape-recorded messages to family members. Ask your wing officer about your rights under this regulation. If they say, "I've never heard of it," persist with your request because this regulation or PSI (Prison Service Instruction) certainly does exist. I know because I made good use of it and gave great joy to my mother by sending her my descriptions of life on the wing. She used to invite her friends around to listen to my "voicemails from prison". You can also send oral messages to your wider circle via family members or close friends who come to visit you.

Finally, if you are so inclined, pray for your family and friends. If you pray for someone you are using a supernatural channel of communication to them. This is a mystery, but millions of prayer transmitters and prayer receivers have discovered that it can work.

To sum up: although you are in prison you are not silenced or exiled. So, use your opportunities for communicating with the outside world to the maximum, and enjoy them to the full. And a piece of good news: at the time of writing it looks as though the Ministry of Justice will soon allow an increasing number of prisoners to send emails. So start writing or communicating today!

EDWARD

On average, it costs about £35,000 to keep someone in prison for one year. Society spends a lot of money to keep you locked up.

However, this is not a good reason to turn your back on society, or to refuse to engage with those around you. Don't give in to anger or bitterness, because you will, sooner or later, become part of wider society again.

You will need people around you when you get out, too. You will have been used to easy, quick communication through the internet and smartphones, and losing this freedom is one of the most difficult aspects of entering prison. Letters can seem agonizingly slow compared to the time it would take on the outside to pick up your phone and fire off a text message. You will have access to telephones, of course, but this access will usually be time-constrained and – to put it mildly – expensive. Most prisoners will have a select few people to whom they make telephone calls: these calls are enormously precious, and it's no wonder that telephone usage is amongst the most common causes of unrest on the wing.

Putting those valuable few minutes on the phone aside, it will be through traditional "snail-mail" that most of your correspondence will happen. Although this might feel like stepping back in time, communicating by letter is an art which you can learn; and it is one which you will have plenty of time to practise. Nowadays, receiving a personal letter is – usually – a pleasure, or at least it signals that the sender has felt that either their news is, or *you* are, important enough to them to warrant the time spent crafting it. People take writing a letter seriously, and you may find that an exchange of letters offers glimpses of meaning and a depth of thought which even – or perhaps especially – a face-to-face conversation would never allow.

As I write this, there sits behind me, on the floor, an old-fashioned trunk which I now use as a coffee-table. Within that trunk there is a box, and within that box a bag. That bag contains every letter I received during my own prison sentence, which averaged out at four or five for every day I was inside – nowhere near Jonathan's total, but still a sizeable amount. Occasionally I clear the top of the trunk of stuff, find the letters, and sit on the floor surrounded by them, reading them.

It is always a highly charged experience.

There are the letters of love and support, support so unconditional that crippling feelings of unworthiness overwhelm me on each rereading as powerfully as the first time I read their lines.

Then there are the letters from people I hadn't spoken to in years, people who often didn't know quite what to say but who felt they wanted to write anyway. I felt more grateful for their letters than they could possibly imagine.

Some letters are shot through with profound, quiet sadness. They are from people who had high hopes for me, who are frustrated, angry, or – worse – just *sad* that I could have been so stupid as to land myself in this situation when I had "so much potential".

And then there are the letters which cause me to wince even now as I unfold them, the letters where the anger rushes up off the page, swirling around me, disorientating me, and filling my ears with noise. They are rare, those letters, but they come from those whose words have the greatest impact, and so they stay in the bag within a box within a trunk, to be excavated and reread when I can't resist picking at that particular scab.

The letters you write and the letters you receive will become part of you. You will be shown compassion for which you might not dare to hope; and you may read words of anger which sadden you, frustrate you, or even anger you in turn. Probably you will write such words, too. But expressing yourself to people outside the prison walls, whatever the emotions are you express, is vital.

Those who care for you *want* to hear from you, just as you want to hear from them.

There may be times when you don't want to have contact with anyone outside; you would rather live privately with your shame, or anger, or sadness. Don't. Those who care for you *want* to hear from you, just as you want to hear from them. "Keep in touch" is a throwaway phrase, but it contains an important truth. Rereading my old letters, it's striking how often this phrase appears, and it's equally striking how genuine it seems each time it does.

So keep in touch.

Keep in touch

Prisons tend to operate a good couple of decades behind everywhere else. Hopefully the next few years will see prisons allow prisoners to send emails, and to have the chance to make telephone calls directly from their cells. For the moment, though, these opportunities are rare. The government accepts that if prisoners stay in touch with their families and friends, they are much less likely to reoffend after release, and email and in-cell calls will help a lot. But all the innovation and technology in the world cannot overcome an individual's own desire to cut themselves off, so please... keep in touch.

"Anxiety weighs down the human heart, but a good word cheers it up" (Proverbs 12:25, NRSV). There will be much weighing on your heart. But do not underestimate the number of people who will be overjoyed to hear from you, and whose good words in response can – and will – gladden your heart as you continue on your journey.

Lord God,

You created us to be social beings, taking comfort from companionship.

Grant me the strength not to close down paths of communication with the outside world; the bravery to accept the hand of friendship from those who offer it; and the courage to ask for help without shame.

Please care for those whose contact with the world outside the walls has withered and died; and for those who want to keep in touch but cannot.

Through Christ our Lord,

Amen.

Chapter 8
Visits

Then the King will say to those on his right, "Come, you who are blessed by my Father; take your inheritance, the kingdom prepared for you since the creation of the world. For I was hungry and you gave me something to eat, I was thirsty and you gave me something to drink, I was a stranger and you invited me in, I needed clothes and you clothed me, I was sick and you looked after me, I was in prison and you came to visit me."

> **Whatever you did for one of the least of these brothers and sisters of mine, you did for me.**

Then the righteous will answer him, "Lord, when did we see you hungry and feed you, or thirsty and give you something to drink? When did we see you a stranger and invite you in, or needing clothes and clothe you? When did we see you sick or in prison and go to visit you?"

The King will reply, "Truly I tell you, whatever you did for one of the least of these brothers and sisters of mine, you did for me." (Matthew 25:34–40, NIV)

This is a famous piece of scripture. But how helpful is it for those in prison? Does it mean rather more to the visitor than the visited? It suggests that in visiting someone in prison, the visitor associates with those Christ deems his brothers and sisters – the neediest, the most unloved in society. How do you feel about that label?

Running through Jesus' words is a sense of *giving*, especially hospitality. The giving of something to drink; of food; of welcome; etc. What do visitors to those in prison *give* today? Time, certainly. But more than that: visiting someone in prison can be emotionally difficult, hard to organize, often undignified, and frequently upsetting. But it is of vital importance, often to the visitor, and always to the visited.

Prison visits are a lifeline to those inside. Both of us found that visits kept us going from week to week.

But lots of people in our prisons never receive a single visitor.

Reflections

JONATHAN

Visits can be the greatest blessings of a prison sentence. But they can be quite complex. Friends and family members can react in odd ways, and like almost everything that happens in prison, reunions in the visiting hall can at first seem strange. Yet this is one area of prison life in which the good heavily outweighs the bad.

The Prison Service takes a lot of trouble to make visits possible, and usually administers them well. This is because the criminal justice system recognizes that allowing a prisoner to have regular human contact with family and friends is a sensible way to encourage a good atmosphere in prison, and gives the prisoner a better chance of going straight after it.

The arrangements for V/Os or Visiting Orders are relatively straightforward, but any new prisoner should make an effort to understand them and work with them. They vary slightly from establishment to establishment but broadly speaking a newly arriving prisoner is issued with a V/O every fourteen days. As a sentence progresses, he or she will be allowed more frequent visits. An enhanced prisoner (someone whose good behaviour has earned them extra privileges) may be able to get a weekly V/O which allows him or her to be visited by three friends or family members per visit. Visits usually last an hour, or as long as two hours in some prisons.

Preparing for a visit can be quite a challenge for both the visitors and the visited. The prisoner will usually try to smarten up in order to look their best, to put on a brave face, and to appear cheerful. This can be difficult when your spirits are at a low ebb. Even so, it is well worth making the effort to be upbeat, because no prisoner wants to worry their nearest and dearest by moaning about the unpleasantness of life behind bars. So try to start the visit on a positive note by saying how great it is to be reunited with family and friends.

Visitors will often have had long and difficult journeys to get to the prison. They can be upset by the queuing, the security procedures, and sometimes by the aggressive searching. I vividly remember how disconcerted my teenage daughters were when they entered HMP Belmarsh for their first visit. They had their gums inspected, their pockets turned out, and the soles of their feet examined. What is a normal routine for a high-security prison with a drug smuggling problem is totally abnormal to an innocent first-time visitor. So allowances may need to be made if the participants on both sides are a little tense and unsettled at the start of a visit.

Conversations during visits can go anywhere, but often everyone is hoping for reassurance. The prisoner longs to hear that their family are just about managing at home without them. Reports of normal life, about how the kids are doing at school, or how the neighbours are asking kindly after them, can be music to an inmate's ears. For their part visiting relatives usually enjoy an "I'm surviving quite well" narrative and humorous stories about the extraordinary characters and customs of prison life. However, the attempts to reassure one another will only partly cover the pain that everyone is likely to be feeling. For every custodial sentence is a sentence on the prisoner's family as well as on the prisoner.

> The attempts to reassure one another will only partly cover the pain that everyone is likely to be feeling.

Months after my release, one of my daughters described to me what happened after we had exchanged goodbyes in the visiting hall. "You would go to the exit and wave to us. Then we would wave back, so enthusiastically and cheerfully," she said. "But five seconds after you were out of sight we would collapse in floods of tears."

Despite the tears and the tensions, visits are hugely beneficial because they keep the bonds of love and friendship alive. They are also an invaluable reminder that there will be life after prison, and that relationships can one day be rebuilt. Even when they seem to go badly, visits keep alight a beacon of hope in a prisoner's heart. I enjoyed almost all my visitors, especially my nearest and dearest. But there was one exception: my mother. Although we loved each other greatly, my 88-year-old mother simply could not bear the sight of her little boy (aged 56!) dressed in a prison uniform. Within moments of my arrival in the visiting hall she would choke up. Then I would choke up too. Getting her visit back on an even keel of tear-free conversation was quite an effort.

The emotional prisoner's mother is a well-known figure to prison officers, who usually go out of their way to treat her, other family members, and the prisoner's friends with kindness and sensitivity.

The only exception to this rule during my sentence came when my old Cabinet colleague Michael Howard came to visit me at HMP Standford Hill. As Home Secretary he had made changes to the pay and conditions of prison officers, sweeping away some of their old customs that had resulted in excessive claims for overtime.

His reforms had not been forgotten by the local branch of the Prison Officers' Association (POA), the trades union for those working in prisons. So they deliberately gave him a hard time, sending him to the back of the queue, aggressively searching him, and treating him and his son Nick quite rudely. The POA's behaviour did not go unnoticed by the prisoners in the visiting hall, who decided to greet the former Home Secretary with elaborate courtesy. Several of them rose to their feet and shook his hand, saying, "Good to see you Mr Howard... Welcome to Standford Hill... Great of you to stick by your old mate." They even applauded him as he left the room with smiles that made an amusing contrast with the sulky frowns of the POA members. Michael took it all in his stride. Prison often has scenes that could have appeared in a *Carry On* film and this was one of them.

Spare a thought or a prayer for the minority of prisoners who get no visits. I will always remember the moment when I was sprucing myself up in the washroom one afternoon. An old lag, a lifer, asked me: "Got a visit, have you Jonno?"

When I nodded, he continued in a plaintive tone, "I haven't had a visit for seventeen years."

Sadly, there are quite a number of lonely prisoners who have been disowned in this way by their families and friends. Some of them do, in the end, get arranged visits from Official Prison Visitors or visitors from excellent charities such as New Bridge (of which I am Vice-President). Such kind visits can give a helpful boost to the morale of unvisited prisoners. They should also serve as a reminder that those who do have friends and family willing to visit them should count their blessings – and remember to thank their visitors.

Prison visits are a bright light shining in the gloom of jail life. So make the most of your visits, and enjoy them to the full, for they will lighten the darkness of your sentence.

EDWARD

If your first few days in prison are anything like mine, you will be able to think of little else but seeing your loved ones as soon as possible. All visits are times of heightened emotion, but that first visit following your disappearance from the dock will be particularly intense.

Do remember, as you wait to be processed into the visits hall, that visiting a prisoner is an unpleasant, lengthy, expensive, and unnerving affair. If your loved one doesn't behave in the way you hope for – in other words, isn't as emotionally stable and strong as you would expect – do not be alarmed. Just as you will still be reeling from the events of the last days and weeks, so will they, and whereas you will have had a short time to begin adjusting to prison life, they will not.

For a variety of reasons, my first visit was not until eight days after my arrival in prison. James, my cellmate whom I introduced in the first chapter, received a "72-hour gate visit" (an initial visit within the first three days of your arrival) to which all new prisoners are entitled. Having been told that prison was unlikely in my case, I had made the mistake of not fully preparing for going to jail. So neither I nor my partner knew about these visits.

James and his family had wisely done their research beforehand. As I watched how this visit on the Sunday afternoon following our Friday evening arrival lifted his mood and calmed him down, it caused me – I'm ashamed to admit – more than a flash of resentment. Eventually, though, my turn came around, and that first visit is a memory which will stay with me for my whole life: a wonderful moment of joy and happiness, shot through with pain as I was forced, for the first time, to look into the eyes of those whom I had failed.

Everyone has a different approach to visits. Jonathan was pleased to receive a veritable *Who's Who* of political and religious figures streaming through the prison gates to see him. By contrast, I struggled to come to terms with the idea that anyone other than my closest friends would see me like this. My sentence was quite short, so it was easier to tell myself that I could tough it out. By and large, it is your decision to make, although it is possible for people to book visits without your knowledge, leaving you in the odd position of walking down to the visits hall with absolutely no idea who will be sat there, nor whether they will have remembered to bring enough pound coins to keep you supplied with the only tea in which you will find real milk during your whole sentence.

Take a moment to glance up during the course of your visit. Looking around you will see the whole breadth of human emotion and interaction. There is a lot of love swirling round those impersonal halls, but there is also a great deal of pain, and frequently anger, too. There will be parents playing with children too young to know where they are; there will be couples talking through the strain that one party's imprisonment is placing on the relationship. There will be arguments and, perhaps worst of all, there will be people sitting silently, nothing left to discuss and no energy left to argue, but fixed in place by a sense that to leave would be abandonment; to walk away from the table would be to walk away from an awful lot more than that.

A bad visit is one of the worst things – day-to-day – that can happen to a prisoner. And, as with all prison life, what would have been considered a very minor disagreement on the outside can seem much worse, looking back, once the cell door is locked for the evening.

There is something you can do here. Keep an eye on those around you and don't hesitate to extend the hand of friendship to anyone who looks distressed on the walk back to your wing. You may be turned down, but that person will know that you noticed, and may yet come back to speak to you.

If you've had a bad visit there's only one thing to do: sleep on it. It will be tempting to fire off letters or sprint to the phone the minute you get back onto the wing. Don't. Your emotions will always be in turmoil after a visit, no matter how well or badly it went. Let things settle down, maybe talk it over with a trusted friend or cellmate, and then sleep on it. It will always seem better in the morning.

Visits – along with letters and phone calls – may well be the fuel which powers you from one week to the next in prison. But that will not be true for everyone. Some people will find themselves in prison far from home. Some people will have been in prison many years, and their friends and family will have dropped away. Some people simply don't have many friends and family to care for them. For these people, watching the majority of the wing disappear for two hours and come back talking of nothing but their visitors can be a dispiriting, painful experience.

Pray for those people who face prison without the weekly reminders of the presence of those who love them. Pray also for all visitors. It is a difficult experience to which they subject themselves out of love – a strong force indeed, and one for which you can truly thank God.

Pray also for all visitors. It is a difficult experience to which they subject themselves out of love.

Be realistic

As both these reflections have emphasized, being visited is almost always the highlight of the week. As we have also both noted, though, visits are often emotionally draining experiences for everyone involved – including for those who have to sit and watch others heading to the visits hall, a walk they may not have made for many years.

Take strength from your visits, then, but be realistic about them: just as not every conversation in everyday life follows the path we might hope for it, so it is with visits. As we have said more than once in this book, perspective is an easy thing to lose in prison – and so a "bad" visit is almost never as bad as it seems in the moment. And although you have every right to rejoice in a happy, enjoyable visit, always do so in the knowledge that there are many for whom your rejoicing will be difficult to watch.

Lord,

Thank you for those who brave the unknown to visit friends or family in prison; and for those whose visits are second nature.

For children seeing without understanding, beginning to understand, or understanding all too well. For parents angry, exasperated, disappointed, or resigned.

To those who find visiting or being visited difficult give courage;

To those who rejoice in their visits give magnanimity;

And upon those who live their lives in prison with no visitors, pour your unfailing, overflowing love that they may draw strength from your presence at their side.

Amen.

Chapter 9
Living and Growing Positively

With the final chapter of this short book, we arrive at its essence.

Previous chapters have covered fairly specific ideas or events: chapel, staff, the first night, etc. They have, if you like, tried to help in the process of bedding in to your new life and building the foundations upon which the rest of your sentence will be built.

This chapter ranges a little further, and, we hope, offers some support as you go through a process which many prisoners never manage, but which is essential if your time in prison is to be fruitful: that is, lifting your gaze from the immediate – the day-by-day – to the journey ahead of you.

That can be quite scary, which is why many don't do it. But this is your chance to make some long-term plans, and to work on your relationships – even your relationship with God. It's one of the main opportunities prison offers you; live out your sentence with your eyes fixed

This is your chance to make some long-term plans, and to work on your relationships – even your relationship with God.

never further than today and tomorrow, and you will serve a very different type of jail-time than that which is within your grasp.

Reflections

JONATHAN

"Be positive!" sounds like a cliché. Putting it into practice while serving a prison sentence can be challenging, to put it mildly. Yet if you fill your life with self-pity, worry, grumbling, and complaining, you will only add to your pain and misery.

But how can anyone be positive and upbeat in a situation where the pressures of prison life are often demoralizing? Here are five practical and spiritual suggestions. They are not as corny as they might seem at first glance.

1. Keep busy
2. Smile!
3. Be a good neighbour
4. Stay cool under pressure
5. Find ways of serving others in the prison community.

1. Keep busy

There's not enough to do in prison. Idleness can all too easily lead to unhappiness. So be a self-starter. Apply for a job that means something. I was a wing cleaner, which mainly meant being a toilet cleaner. It sounded rather demeaning at first. But, in reality, keeping the showers, loos, and urinals hygienic is a really important task in a prison where smells and potential infections can be unpleasant.

I felt enormously chuffed when one of the "Big Faces" visited from another wing and told me: "I came over here to piss, Jonno, because you keep the cleanest bogs in the gaff!" An unusual compliment to my skills with the wire brush, plunger, and Harpic, but the work kept me busy and the toilets spick and span.

Separating the worthwhile jobs from the pointless ones is a valuable exercise. So is the quest for other interesting activities. The range of educational or vocational courses is often rather good. Think about learning a foreign language, upgrading your computer skills, or even getting a degree in the subject of your choice if you are serving a longish sentence.

If you look around you and ask questions in the education department, or approach sympathetic officers, you can soon find alternatives to sleeping, playing Kalooki, or more self-destructive ways of passing the time.

2. Smile!

This sounds a really cheesy suggestion. Maybe it is. Yet it is still the best way of communicating that you have an alert mind and a pleasant spirit. If you spread a little sunshine on the wing by your cheerful demeanour you may be surprised by the good responses you get.

There is a lot of laughter on a prison journey. Intentional and unintentional comedians flourish in the theatre of the absurd that a jail creates. You will meet larger-than-life characters who could have come from a sitcom. Enjoy them! Prison humour has its own language and its own distinctive feel of black comedy. Laugh along with the flow of it and you will lighten the darkness of your time behind bars.

3. Be a good neighbour

This is a good way to stay positive. I found the milk of human kindness flowed surprisingly well and warmly in all three of the jails where I served my sentence.

So go out of your way to be kind and helpful to anyone who has had a knock-back, or looks sad and gloomy, or who seems bewildered by their new environment. Very young or old prisoners are particularly vulnerable. They really appreciate a friendly word or a helping hand.

> **Very young or old prisoners are particularly vulnerable. They really appreciate a friendly word or a helping hand.**

Everyone's heard the jingle "good neighbours become good friends". It is truer of prisoners than many other kinds of neighbour. Friendships deepened by the adversity of sharing life together on a wing can be enduring and satisfying.

As a small illustration of this, when I was ordained in St Paul's Cathedral in 2018, six of my wing neighbours from HMP Belmarsh in 1999 came to the service and the party afterwards. An interesting example of how good prison neighbours become good friends.

4. Stay cool under pressure

This is easier said than done when a spice-filled inmate is kicking off on the wing, causing association to be cancelled and everyone having to go back to their cells.

Such pressures and provocations are a big part of prison life.

There's a good line from Rudyard Kipling's poem "If" which goes:

> If you can keep your head when all about you
> Are losing theirs and blaming it on you...

It is useful advice to follow to achieve peace in your own mind and peace on the wing. It also points to a sensible and surprising prison truth.

An unwritten and unspoken fact of jail life is that prison only becomes bearable if officers and inmates cooperate together, with sensible attitudes of give and take. If everyone kicked off each time they felt frustrated, antsy, or angry, our jails would be in a permanent state of uproar. Prison relies on moderate behaviour by people with cool heads. So stay cool!

5. Find ways of serving others in the prison community

There are special opportunities for such service. They include being "Listeners" (Samaritans-trained counsellors), mediators, wing information advisers, fire watchers, and chapel orderlies. Another interesting opportunity is to become a "Toe by Toe" instructor. This is a task for prisoners with good literary skills to coach prisoners in the three Rs so that they escape from the disadvantage of illiteracy. Lives are being transformed by "Toe by Toe" so it is a wonderful community service activity. Wing officers in the education department can guide you if you want to find out more.

EDWARD

What do we mean when we use the verb "to live"?

If I tell someone that "I am living," I might just be stating the obvious: I am alive; I am not dead. I am surviving. But if, with a glint in my eye and an emphasis in the right place, I tell them "I am *living*!" then the meaning changes. I might mean that I am – as I see it – making the most of the few short years we are all afforded on this earth: I am "living life to the full".

As you look around your prison, you might be forgiven for thinking that there's a lot of "existing" going on, and not a lot of "living". "Keep your head down and just get through" was the most common piece of advice given to me in the early days of my own prison sentence, and it's not bad advice to follow while you find your feet and begin to understand the rhythm of prison life.

But if you follow it to the letter, throughout your entire sentence, then you will have missed an opportunity. Your mind

Your mind doesn't have to be trapped along with your body.

doesn't have to be trapped along with your body. Your life hasn't stopped as a result of being sent to prison. The courts cannot physically remove the months and years that were mentioned at your sentencing – they can only dictate where you spend them.

Those months and years, though, can be months and years of anger and resentment, bitterness and pain; they can be months and years which you can regard as *lost* –

wasted – irretrievable; *irredeemable*. You will see many people for whom this is true. They are prisoners twice over: prisoners in their body and prisoners in their mind. They are crippled by inwardly directed anger and shame, and those toxins slowly destroy their ability to look to the future. Anger and shame can also stop them opening themselves to God.

This is not to say that you must aim for some sort of calm, passive state of enlightenment, mind detached entirely from the bodily reality of your situation. Anger with yourself can be productive, and God knows we are often angry with him.

In one of my favourite episodes of any television programme ever made – "Two Cathedrals", the season two finale of *The West Wing* – President of the United States Jed Bartlet, a devout, God-fearing man, stands alone in Washington National Cathedral after the funeral of his long-time friend and secretary Mrs Landingham, and rails – screams, even – at God. Finally he lights a cigarette only to throw it to the floor of the cathedral and stamp it out with his foot.

Which of us hasn't felt that sort of anger with God? Former Dean of Westminster Michael Mayne wrote a short book reflecting on a year he spent suffering with ME, called *A Year Lost and Found*. In it, he talks of anger with God, and reminds the reader: "At Calvary

God offers love for our rage; compassion for our hate.

God in Christ invites us to vent our anger and our rage upon him, in order that we may discover in him a love that is stronger than our hate." With the infinite patience of the sort of parent we all aspire to be, God offers love for our rage; compassion for our hate.

The best, most meaningful relationships are those where nothing – no emotion, no sentiment – needs to be concealed. That is the sort of relationship offered to us by God, far surpassing all human relationships with their resentments and jealousy. God's love for us is assured, but his hopes for us can only start to come true when we open ourselves – make ourselves vulnerable – to that terrifying sort of love where nothing is ever demanded.

That's a tall order at the best of times. In prison, it is harder still, and yet also, somehow, infinitely easier: there is less to lose for most of us when in prison than at any other time in our life; we have already been stripped down to the barest of states, perhaps our lowest ebb. Crawling to God on your hands and knees isn't a bad place to start.

In that same book I mentioned a few lines ago, Michael Mayne reproduces part of a poem by Caryll Houselander:

> *There is a young man*
> *who lives in a world of progress.*
> *He used to worship a God*
> *Who was kind to him.*
> *The God had a long, white beard.*
> *He lived in the clouds.*
> *But, all the same,*
> *He was close to the solemn child*
> *who had secretly shut him up in a picture book*
> *[...]*
> *If he had only known that the God in the picture book*
> *is not an old man in the clouds,*

but the seed of life in his soul;
the man would have lived,
and his life would have flowered
with the flower of limitless joy.
But he does not know,
and in him
the Holy Ghost
is a poor little bird
in a cage,
who never sings
and never opens his wings,
yet never, never
desires to be gone away.

This is the heart of the matter. God "never, never desires to be gone away". Wherever we are, whatever we have done, he is there for us; for you. In amidst the noise and hubbub of the prison and of your own mind it is easy to overlook the caged bird. You cannot open the door to your cell, but you can open the door of that cage, let the little bird unfurl its stiffened wings, and with them enfold your heart. It doesn't take much, but it is the key to living – the key to real, free, flowering, joyful *life*. That may seem a distant prospect as you read these lines. But even if, as former Dean of Durham Michael Sadgrove asserts:

... overwhelmed by pain, or the threat of disaster, or the memory of betrayal, all we can manage is the psalmist's final whisper, "but I will trust in you", the God who is enthroned from of old will assure us that it is enough.

Help me to find the good

Generous God,

Your will for us is that our lives might be filled with joy and happiness.

In this place where both seem in short supply, help me to find the good in those who have buried it deeply; to see the beauty even where it is well hidden; to hear the laughter as quiet as it may be; and through this, aware of your presence with me, to live a life of love and joyfulness.

Amen.

Conclusion

Serving a prison sentence is full of contradictions.

Just as sometimes life in a large city can be unbearably lonely, so you can be lonely in prison.

Another contradiction is that prison doesn't just affect the prisoner. Just as the stone plopping into the pond has no idea of the ripples it causes, your intensely private experience of doing time will continue to impact your loved ones in ways which you will go on discovering for years after you've left the prison gate at the end of your sentence.

You can add another contradiction. You can take an experience which for many is spent desperately trying to make time pass more quickly, and you can fashion from it a period of your life which, somewhere down the line, you might not recoil from remembering; which you might not see as a tragic "lost" few months or years.

Prison doesn't have to be that. Your time in prison is as real as the time you have spent – and will spend – back in the outside world. Few of us would choose it, but you don't have to waste it. "Killing time" is a throwaway phrase, one we use every day while standing in a queue or on listening to hold music. Apply it to months and years, though, and it is a horrifying thought. It may sound trite, or it may sound ridiculous, but a sentence like the one served by you, or your loved one, or your friend, is an opportunity.

Men and women down the ages have done remarkable things with their time in prison – and there is nothing more remarkable than opening your heart to God's love.

Men and women down the ages have done remarkable things with their time in prison

There's a famous painting by William Holman Hunt which hangs in Keble College, Oxford; and a larger reproduction of it hangs in St Paul's Cathedral in London. It is called *The Light of the World*.

In it, Jesus is knocking on a door. The door has no handle, no keyhole, and is overgrown with vegetation; it has never been opened, and it cannot be opened from the outside. This door is the human soul, and Christ asks permission to enter.

So here's another contradiction. In prison, as you stare at your cell door, you see no handle and no keyhole. It is not yours to open and, with keys, those on the outside can come in at will. You are confined to that space, and yet it is never quite yours. But the door to your heart; the door to your soul: this is the only door that matters, and only you can open it. And if you do, there is no question: Christ will be there, knuckles raw from knocking and tears of joy on his cheeks that you have invited him in.

This book can only hope to have shed some light on the door. But it is written by two people who, at one time or another, reached out, lifted the latch, and stood face-to-face with Christ waiting outside. Only you can lift that latch, but the words we have written will, we pray, give you the courage to do so. Once you have done, you may in time start finding ways of showing others their own dusty, neglected door.

As you, or your loved ones, negotiate a prison sentence, know that the prayers of many are with you, and that our Lord, ever-loving, is at your side for each and every step of the daunting journey on which you have set out.